Mary Danby

KT-116-449

# How Trivial
# Can You Get?

An Armada Original

*How Trivial Can You Get?*
was first published in the U.K. in Armada
in 1986 by Fontana Paperbacks,
8 Grafton Street, London W1X 3LA.

Armada is an imprint of
Fontana Paperbacks, part of
the Collins Publishing Group.

Printed and bound in Great Britain by
William Collins Sons & Co. Ltd., Glasgow.

# How to play an exciting quiz game with this book

**The object of the game is to be the first to reach the middle of the book. Players ask each other questions from both the back and front of the book. The answers can be found on the back of each question page.**

Each player should have a bookmark.

## For two players
One player chooses an **odd** number between 1 and 15, and answers questions from the **front** of the book.
The other player chooses an **even** number between 2 and 16, and answers questions from the **back** of the book.

Toss a coin to see who should begin.

- Players answer **only** the questions that bear the number they have chosen.
- Work from the outside of the book towards the centre.
- When a player answers a question correctly, he has another turn.
- When a player answers a question incorrectly, his turn is over.

* If a player answers an "A" question correctly, he goes straight on to the next quiz.
* If a player answers an "A" question incorrectly, he stays on the same quiz and tries to answer the "B" question on his next turn.
* If a player answers a "B" question correctly, he goes straight on to the next quiz.
* If a player answers a "B" question incorrectly, he goes on to the next quiz on his next turn.

Use bookmarks to help you remember which quiz you have reached. -

**The first player to reach the centre is the winner.**

## For more than 2 players

Each player chooses a number, as before, but there should be as many odd numbers as even. This way, the players with odd numbers ask questions of those with even numbers, and vice versa. They thus don't get to see their own answers.

**1A** What name is given to an arena for ice- or roller-skating?

**1B** Who was Enrico Caruso?

---

**3A** What does the Russian word "Dah" mean?

**3B** Which band of men was played by film actors Yul Brynner, Steve McQueen, Charles Bronson, Horst Buchholz, Robert Vaughn, Brad Dexter and James Coburn?

---

**5A** What birds cackle and honk? ✓

**5B** *Piste, schuss, langlauf* and stem Christie are all terms connected with which sport?

---

**7A** Which fictional governess flew with the aid of an umbrella? ✓

**7B** How many colours are there in a rainbow?

---

**9A** What does a choreographer create?

**9B** If your hobby was campanology, would you collect postcards, go hiking, ring bells or make baskets?

---

**11A** Whose motto is "Lend a Hand"? ✓

**11B** Chippendale and Hepplewhite are both styles of —what?

---

**13A** What is the natural food of a cormorant? ✓

**13B** How many edges has a cube?

---

**15A** What is another name for a cradle song?

**15B** Which one of these is extinct: bison, albatross, great auk, zebu? ✓

# Mixed Bag

**1A** A rink.
**1B** A singer. (A famous operatic tenor.)

---

**3A** Yes.
**3B** The Magnificent Seven.

---

**5A** Geese.
**5B** Ski-ing.

---

**7A** Mary Poppins.
**7B** Seven.

---

**9A** Dances.
**9B** Ring bells.

---

**11A** The Brownies'.
**11B** Furniture.

---

**13A** Fish.
**13B** Twelve.

---

**15A** A lullaby.
**15B** Great auk.

**1A** What is Scooby Doo's nephew called?

**1B** In *Dallas*, what is the name of J.R.'s son? ✓

**3A** What does Popeye eat to give him strength?

**3B** In the television series *Airwolf*, what is the name of the actor who plays Stringfellow Hawke?

**5A** In *Crossroads*, which character nearly always wears a woolly hat?

**5B** Which well-known male dancer stars in *The Hot Shoe Show?*

**7A** Nicholson, Humphries, Gall and Somerville—what do they do?

**7B** In which TV programme does a character have a zip for a mouth? ✓

**9A** What colour is the *Jim'll Fix It* medal ribbon?

**9B** On which day of the week is *Top of the Pops?*

**11A** Which TV programme features Cousin Daisy, Uncle Jesse and Boss Hogg?

**11B** What is Spiderman's real name?

**13A** In *Diff'rent Strokes*, what is the name of Arnold's brother?

**13B** On which sport does Dan Maskell commentate?

**15A** In which TV programme can you do the Gold Run?

**15B** What is the name of the pub featured in *East Enders?*

**1A** Scrappy Doo.
**1B** John Ross.

---

**3A** Spinach.
**3B** Jan Michael Vincent.

---

**5A** Benny.
**5B** Wayne Sleep.

---

**7A** They're newsreaders.
**7B** *Rainbow*. (Zippy.)

---

**9A** Red.
**9B** Thursday.

---

**11A** *The Dukes of Hazzard*.
**11B** Peter Parker.

---

**13A** Willis.
**13B** Tennis.

---

**15A** *Blockbusters*.
**15B** The Queen Victoria.

# Animals

**Q**

1A   Highwayman Dick Turpin had a famous horse. What was its name?

1B   Which animal comes first in a dictionary? ✓ .

---

3A   How many lives is a cat supposed to have? ✓

3B   What type of animal is a pipistrelle? ✓

---

5A   Which country do budgerigars originally come from? ✓

5B   What breed of sheepdog is the film star Lassie?

---

7A   A Belgian hare is not a hare. What is it?

7B   What might be common, palmate, crested or marbled?

---

9A   Is a capuchin a lizard, a bear or a monkey?

9B   What is a female fox called?

---

11A   A thick-bodied British snake, less than 60 cms long, with a dark zig-zag pattern and a poisonous bite —what is it?

11B   What is another name for an elk?

---

13A   How many teats are there on a cow's udder?

13B   What is the name of the famous London sanctuary for dogs? ✓

---

15A   A mule is a cross between a donkey and a—what?

15B   What kind of animal is Beatrix Potter's Mrs Tiggiewinkle?

# Animals

1A  Black Bess.
1B  The aardvark.

3A  Nine.
3B  A bat.

5A  Australia.
5B  Collie.

7A  A rabbit.
7B  A newt.

9A  A monkey.
9B  A vixen.

11A  An adder (viper).
11B  Moose.

13A  Four.
13B  Battersea Dogs' Home.

15A  A horse.
15B  A hedgehog.

# Food & Drink

**1A** What is traditionally eaten on Shrove Tuesday? ✓

**1B** Sarsaparilla—is it a fish dish, a drink, or a kind of fruit sauce?

---

**3A** What are whitebait?

**3B** Mange-tout, kohlrabi, okra and kale are all what?

---

**5A** What type of meat is normally used in moussaka?

**5B** Apart from bread, what is the principal ingredient of Welsh rarebit?

---

**7A** What is the wine called *sake* made from?

**7B** In a restaurant, might you be offered *hors d'oeuvres* as a first course, a main course or a dessert?

---

**9A** What traditional national dish is made from various ingredients stuffed into a sheep's stomach?

**9B** In which country is paella frequently served?

---

**11A** What are tied together to make a bouquet garni?

**11B** Before turkeys were introduced into Britain, what was traditionally eaten at Christmas?

---

**13A** According to tradition, which food should be eaten only when there is an R in the month?

**13B** Capuccino and espresso are ways of serving—what?

---

**15A** What type of meal might begin with prawn crackers? ✓

**15B** Cob-nut is another name for—what?

13

# Food & Drink

**1A** Pancakes.
**1B** A drink.

---

**3A** Very small fish.
**3B** Vegetables.

---

**5A** Lamb.
**5B** Cheese.

---

**7A** Rice.
**7B** As a first course.

---

**9A** Haggis.
**9B** Spain.

---

**11A** Herbs.
**11B** Goose.

---

**13A** Oysters.
**13B** Coffee.

---

**15A** A Chinese meal.
**15B** Hazelnut.

# Myths & Legends

**1A**  The Roman king of the sea was Neptune. What was his Greek name?

**1B**  Did the Greek gods drink nectar, mead or grape juice?

**3A**  Anubis, Osiris, Isis, Amen-Ra and Nut—where were these gods once worshipped?

**3B**  In the Trojan War, what device did the Greeks use to get inside the walls of Troy?

**5A**  What is the connection between Ulysses and Odysseus?

**5B**  Which goddess was known as the huntress?

**7A**  Whose punishment was to carry the sky on his shoulders?

**7B**  Theseus killed a monster that was half man and half — what?

**9A**  Which Knight of the Round Table fell in love with Queen Guinevere?

**9B**  For how many nights did Scheherazade tell her stories of the Arabian Nights? Was it one hundred and one, one thousand and one or one million and one?

**11A**  What strange power did King Midas have? ✓

**11B**  Who had wings on his heels?

**13A**  How many heads had the dog Cerberus who guarded the entrance to the underworld?

**13B**  After which Norse god was Thursday named?

**15A**  What modern expression comes from the name of the old ✓ African god Mama Dyumbo?

**15B**  Did the sorceress Circe turn Odysseus' crew into pigs, donkeys, frogs or mice?

# Myths & Legends

1A  Poseidon.
1B  Nectar.

3A  Egypt.
3B  A wooden horse.

5A  They're the same person.
5B  Diana (Artemis).

7A  Atlas's.
7B  Bull.

9A  Sir Lancelot.
9B  One thousand and one.

11A  Everything he touched turned to gold.
11B  Mercury (Hermes).

13A  Three.
13B  Thor.

15A  Mumbo jumbo.
15B  Pigs.

# Colours

**1A** What colour do you get if you mix red, blue and green?

**1B** If you are sad, you are said to be feeling—what colour?

---

**3A** What colour is the bonnet of Noddy's car?

**3B** What name is given to the yellow-green-brown colour used for military uniforms?

---

**5A** What colour is a US passport?

**5B** Cats of one particular colour are always male? Which colour?

---

**7A** What colour is jet?

**7B** In the song, what colour ribbon was tied round an old oak tree?

---

**9A** What colour flag is waved at the end of a motor race?

**9B** In India, what colour is traditionally worn by brides?

---

**11A** What does verdant mean?

**11B** What colour is associated with Communism?

---

**13A** The All Blacks are a rugby team. Where do they come from?

**13B** Which colour does the romantic novelist Barbara Cartland usually wear?

---

**15A** What colour is something that has been gilded?

**15B** If you were titian-haired, would your hair be blonde, red, black or mousey?

# Colours

**1A** Brown.
**1B** Blue.

**3A** Yellow.
**3B** Khaki.

**5A** Green.
**5B** Ginger (Orange).

**7A** Black.
**7B** Yellow.

**9A** Black and white.
**9B** Red.

**11A** Green.
**11B** Red.

**13A** New Zealand.
**13B** Pink.

**15A** Gold.
**15B** Red.

18

# Pop Music

1A  Which singer was rescued when his ocean-going yacht *Drum* capsized?

1B  Who sang "I Know Him So Well" with Elaine Paige?

3A  Which song contains the words "I'm gonna live for ever"?

3B  What nationality is disc jockey Kid Jensen?

5A  Which group was composed of singers called Benny, Bjorn, Frida and Agnetha?

5B  Neil Diamond and Barbra Streisand sang "You don't bring me . . ."—what?

7A  Which famous singer did Shakin' Stevens portray on stage?

7B  Whose last big hit was "Imagine"?

9A  Which pop star co-wrote "Do They Know It's Christmas?" with Bob Geldof?

9B  What is Madonna's real Christian name?  ✓

11A  Which Scottish pop singer had a hit called "Sailing"?

11B  What do these singers all have in common: Phil Collins, Peter Skellern, Elton John, Barry Manilow?  ✓

13A  How many Thompson twins are there?

13B  Whose initials give the Bee Gees their name?

15A  Which famous song by Bill Haley & the Comets begins "One, two, three o'clock"?

15B  Who made a famous video about vampires, werewolves and zombies?

# Pop Music

**1A**  Simon Le Bon.
**1B**  Barbara Dickson.

**3A**  "Fame".
**3B**  Canadian.

**5A**  Abba.
**5B**  Flowers.

**7A**  Elvis Presley.
**7B**  John Lennon's.

**9A**  Midge Ure.
**9B**  Madonna.

**11A**  Rod Stewart.
**11B**  They all play the piano.

**13A**  Three.
**13B**  Barry Gibb.

**15A**  "Rock Around the Clock."
**15B**  Michael Jackson (for his song "Thriller").

# I Say, I Say

**1A** Whose catchphrase is "Nice to see you—to see you, nice"?

**1B** Napoleon said, "An army marches on its . . .'—what?

**3A** "Please, sir, I want some more!" Who said that?

**3B** Which famous film star said, "I want to be alone"?

**5A** In which TV programme does Ruth Madoc say "Hello campers"?

**5B** Whose catchphrase was "Just like that"?

**7A** Which French queen is supposed to have said, "Let them eat cake"?

**7B** Who sat in the middle of the road saying "Poop, poop"?

**9A** According to Shakespeare, which English king said, "A horse, a horse, my kingdom for a horse"?

**9B** Who said, "That's one small step for a man, one giant leap for mankind"?

**11A** Who is supposed to have said, "Kiss me, Hardy," as he lay dying?

**11B** Which beer is said to refresh the parts that others can't reach?

**13A** Who said, "We shall defend our island, whatever the cost may be"?

**13B** Welsh singer and comedian Max Boyce has a catchphrase. What is it?

**15A** Whose motto was "One for all, and all for one"?

**15B** Cream cakes are said to be "naughty but . . .'—what?

# I Say, I Say

**1A** Bruce Forsyth's.
**1B** Stomach.

**3A** Oliver Twist.
**3B** Greta Garbo.

**5A** *Hi-De-Hi*.
**5B** Tommy Cooper's.

**7A** Marie Antoinette.
**7B** Toad (in *The Wind in the Willows* by Kenneth Grahame).

**9A** Richard III.
**9B** Neil Armstrong (about his first step on the moon).

**11A** Lord Nelson.
**11B** Heineken.

**13A** Sir Winston Churchill.
**13B** "I was there."

**15A** The Three Musketeers'.
**15B** Nice.

# Buildings

**1A** What name is given to a large country house in France?

**1B** Would an old, half-timbered house most likely be Victorian, Regency, Tudor or Edwardian?

---

**3A** What is an underground chamber in a church called?

**3B** In what type of building might you find a portcullis?

---

**5A** What is the area at the top of a flight of stairs known as?

**5B** In which Italian city is the famous Leaning Tower?

---

**7A** What is the headquarters of the Metropolitan Police called?

**7B** Where are the Crown Jewels kept?

---

**9A** What is the name of the official residence of the President of the United States?

**9B** Casement, sash, leaded and dormer are all types of—what?

---

**11A** What is a semi-detached house?

**11B** There is a famous maze in the garden of which Thames-side palace?

---

**13A** What is a chalet made of?

**13B** In which London palace do the Prince and Princess of Wales live?

---

**15A** What would you expect to do in an anteroom—sleep, wait, play games or be ill?

**15B** In building, what is a reinforced steel joist better known as?

# Buildings

1A  A château.
1B  Tudor.

3A  The crypt.
3B  A castle.

5A  The landing.
5B  Pisa.

7A  New Scotland Yard.
7B  In the Tower of London.

9A  The White House.
9B  Window.

11A  One that is joined on one side to another house.
11B  Hampton Court.

13A  Wood.
13B  Kensington Palace.

15A  Wait.
15B  An R.S.J.

24

# Words

1A What is "Mrs" short for?

1B Which English county is sometimes shortened to Salop?

3A What does the word "feline" refer to? ✔

3B "Lingo" is a slang word for—what?

5A What six-letter word means "to preserve in vinegar or brine"?

5B If you asked a French chef for *pommes frites*, what would you get?

7A What is the wife of a maharajah called?

7B Cat, mouse, hamster, horse—which one of these words is polysyllabic?

9A What does the Italian word *bella* mean?

9B How many years does a centenary commemorate?

11A What does "obese" mean?

11B Which form of transport has a name that means "three wheels"?

13A What kind of young animal is known as a joey?

13B Is "pick" a synonym for "chick", "choose", "kip" or "picket"?

15A How would you say "dog" in backslang?

15B Why is a hamburger so called?

# Words

**1A** Mistress.

**1B** Shropshire.

---

**3A** Cats.

**3B** Language.

---

**5A** Pickle.

**5B** Chips.

---

**7A** A maharanee.

**7B** Hamster. (It has more than one syllable.)

---

**9A** Beautiful.

**9B** One hundred.

---

**11A** Very fat.

**11B** Tricycle.

---

**13A** A kangaroo.

**13B** Choose.

---

**15A** God.

**15B** Because it originated in the German city of Hamburg.

# Q

1A  Which snooker player has the nickname "Hurricane"?

1B  In which French town is a 24-hour motor race held?

3A  Which British athlete won a gold medal in the decathlon in both the 1980 and 1984 Olympics?

3B  Hurley, a form of hockey, is played in which country?

5A  Which famous three-day event takes place each year at the home of the Duke of Beaufort?

5B  The Cresta Run is a famous track used in which sport?

7A  Which well-known swimmer is completely bald? √

7B  The footballer Pele played for which country?

9A  Which famous steeplechase is run at Aintree, near Liverpool?

9B  What is the full name of the football club known as "Spurs"?

11A  For what are David Gower, Don Bradman and W.G. Grace famous?

11B  Which sport is played at St. Andrews in Scotland?

13A  How many goals did Gary Lineker score for England in the 1986 World Cup in Mexico?

13B  In which town were both Jayne Torvill and Christopher Dean born?

15A  What is known as the "Sport of Kings"?

15B  What does a boxer wear in his mouth?

# Sport

**1A** Alex Higgins.
**1B** Le Mans.

---

**3A** Daley Thompson.
**3B** Eire.

---

**5A** Badminton Horse Trials.
**5B** Bobsleighing.

---

**7A** Duncan Goodhew.
**7B** Brazil.

---

**9A** The Grand National.
**9B** Tottenham Hotspur.

---

**11A** Playing cricket.
**11B** Golf.

---

**13A** Six.
**13B** Nottingham.

---

**15A** Horse racing.
**15B** A gumshield (mouthpiece).

# Q

1A  Which of these places is not fictional: Narnia, Timbuktu, Atlantis?

1B  What is the national symbol of Canada?

3A  Which African country used to be called Abyssinia—was it Ethiopia, the Sudan or Algeria?

3B  Macgillicuddy's Reeks—are they rocks, lakes, mountains or bogs?

5A  What is the British name for Las Malvinas?

5B  Which ocean does the River Amazon flow into?

7A  The durian comes from Malaysia. Is it a dance, a kind of robe, a fruit or a harp?

7B  In which European country is "Legoland"?  ✓

9A  What do the Americans keep at Fort Knox?

9B  Is the mazurka a national dance of Poland, Hungary, Czechoslovakia or Rumania?

11A  What do the Chinook, the Mistral and the Sirocco have in common?

11B  In what Scottish city is the hill known as Arthur's Seat?

13A  What country does Paddington Bear come from?

13B  Which island is sometimes called "The Emerald Isle"?

15A  The four main Channel Islands are Alderney, Jersey, Sark and—what?

15B  In which country is there a state called the Northern Territory?

**1A** Timbuktu.
**1B** The maple leaf.

**3A** Ethiopia.
**3B** Mountains.

**5A** The Falkland Islands.
**5B** The Atlantic.

**7A** A fruit.
**7B** Denmark.

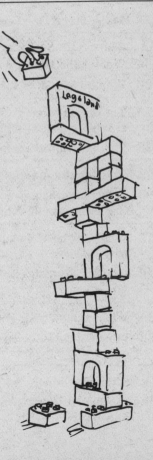

**9A** Gold.
**9B** Poland.

**11A** They are all winds.
**11B** Edinburgh.

**13A** Peru.
**13B** Ireland.

**15A** Guernsey.
**15B** Australia.

# Books ✓

**1A** In Enid Blyton's *Famous Five* books, one of the five is not a person. What is he?

**1B** Who was married to Queen Celeste?

---

**3A** Which school did Elinor M. Brent-Dyer write about?

**3B** In the Winnie-the-Pooh books, who has a Gloomy Place?

---

**5A** Who was the Swiss doctor who made a living creature out of dead bodies?

**5B** Ratty and Mole are characters in which children's book?

---

**7A** Who was imprisoned in a cage in a gingerbread house?

**7B** What or who is Bilbo Baggins?

---

**9A** Which books by Mary Morton feature a little girl called Arrietty?

**9B** Who wrote the James Bond novels?

---

**11A** Gulliver visited a land inhabited by tiny people. What was it called?

**11B** In which book can you find Hazel, Blackberry, Bigwig and Fiver?

---

**13A** Who had a servant called Man Friday?

**13B** In which boys' movement are the group leaders named after *Jungle Book* characters?

---

**15A** Sir Percy Blakeney was known as—what?

**15B** Who wrote the famous book about a horse called Black Beauty?

# Books

**1A** A dog. (Timmy.)
**2B** Babar the elephant.

---

**3A** The Chalet School.
**3B** Eeyore.

---

**5A** Baron Frankenstein.
**5B** *The Wind in the Willows*.

---

**7A** Hansel (in *Hansel & Gretel*).
**7B** A hobbit (in Tolkein's *The Lord of the Rings*).

---

**9A** The *Borrowers* series.
**9B** Ian Fleming.

---

**11A** Lilliput.
**11B** *Watership Down*.

---

**13A** Robinson Crusoe.
**13B** The Cubs (Cub Scouts).

---

**15A** The Scarlet Pimpernel.
**15B** Anna Sewell.

# Science

Q

1A What was an alchemist?

1B Boiling point on the Celsius scale is 100°. What is it on the Centigrade scale?

3A What is the coloured part of the eye called?

3B It might be 40-watt, 60-watt or 100-watt. What is it?

5A What is glass made of?

5B For what kind of exploration is Jacques Cousteau famous?

7A What do you call a three-dimensional image produced by light beams?

7B Ammonia, ether, krypton and neon are all types of—what?

9A What does a lepidopterist study?

9B Does "igneous" refer to rock, lizards or gas?

11A Meteorology—is it the study of space, the weather or proteins?

11B Is a joule a measurement of weight, energy or quantity?

13A What is an aquamarine?

13B How many bytes has a 180K RAM computer?

15A What common name is given to light amplification by stimulated emission of radiation?

15B Is nitrous oxide known as laughing gas, sneezing gas or crying gas?

# Science

A

**1A** Someone who tried to turn base metal into gold.
**1B** 100°. (Centigrade is another name for Celsius.)

---

**3A** The iris.
**3B** An electric light bulb.

---

**5A** Sand.
**5B** Underwater.

---

**7A** A hologram.
**7B** Gas.

---

**9A** Moths and butterflies.
**9B** Rock.

---

**11A** The weather.
**11B** Energy.

---

**13A** A gem stone.
**13B** 180,000.

---

**15A** Laser.
**15B** Laughing gas.

34

# Numbers

1A  There are 7 bones in the human neck. How many are there in a giraffe's neck?

1B  How many years are there in a decade?

---

3A  In the television programme *Blue Peter*, how many regular presenters are there?

3B  How many states make up the United States of America?

---

5A  How many eyelashes does Minnie Mouse have on each upper eyelid?

5B  In the Roman army, how many men did a centurion command?

---

7A  Dr Who has more than one heart. How many altogether?

7B  How many signs of the Zodiac are there?

---

9A  In the song "The Twelve Days of Christmas", how many gold rings were sent by "my true love"?

9B  How many players are there in a Rugby League team?

---

11A  How many engines has Concorde?

11B  The Bible says that man shall live three score years and ten. How many years is this?

---

13A  Fred Trueman took a record number of wickets in Test cricket. Was it 100, 200, 300 or 400?

13B  How many queens of England have been called Anne?

---

15A  How many days after Easter Sunday is Ascension Day?

15B  In *Little Women*, how many sisters are there?

# Numbers

1A  Seven.
1B  Ten.

3A  Three.
3B  Fifty.

5A  Three.
5B  One hundred.

7A  Two.
7B  Twelve.

9A  Five.
9B  Thirteen.

11A  Four.
11B  Seventy.

13A  Three hundred.
13B  Six.

15A  Forty.
15B  Four.

# People

Q

1A  Which famous girl athlete runs barefoot?

1B  Who is the patron saint of travellers?

3A  What do these people have in common: Christie, Crippen, Sutcliffe, Brady?

3B  Whose plot does Bonfire Night commemorate?

5A  Who sailed in the *Golden Hind*?

5B  Which famous German composer was deaf?

7A  One of Robin Hood's Merry Men was known by a name that made a joke about his great height. Who was he?

7B  Which famous dress designer was a Barnardo boy?

9A  In which Italian city was Florence Nightingale born?

9B  Harry S. Truman was the 33rd President of the United States. What did the S. stand for?

11A  For what is Yehudi Menuhin most famous?

11B  The Czar of Russia's notorious adviser Rasputin was known as "The Mad . . ."—what?

13A  What is Cliff Richard's real name? Is it Larry Perkins, John Biggs, Richard Clive or Harry Webb?

13B  Before taking up politics, was Hitler a shopkeeper, a lawyer or a house painter?

15A  Houdini—was he a famous cook, an inventor or an escape artist?

15B  Which famous cricketer walked from John O'Groats to Land's End to raise money for charity?

# People

**1A** Zola Budd.

**1B** St Christopher.

---

**3A** They all are, or were, murderers.

**3B** Guy Fawkes's. (His plot to blow up the Houses of Parliament.)

---

**5A** Sir Francis Drake.

**5B** Beethoven.

---

**7A** Little John.

**7B** Bruce Oldfield.

---

**9A** Florence.

**9B** Nothing. It was just an initial.

---

**11A** Playing the violin.

**11B** Monk.

---

**13A** Harry Webb.

**13B** A house painter.

**15A** An escape artist.

**15B** Ian Botham.

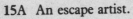

# Plants

**1A** What colour is a celandine? ✓

**1B** Which furry animal lives on eucalyptus leaves? ╱

---

**3A** What is a Webb's Wonder?

**3B** If you squeeze an antirrhinum, its "jaws" will open wide. What is its nickname?

---

**5A** A bunch of this fruit is sometimes called a "hand". What is it?

**5B** Is woodbine another name for ivy, bindweed, heather or honeysuckle?

---

**7A** What are secateurs?

**7B** The horse chestnut tree bears a hard, inedible fruit. What is the common name of this fruit?

---

**9A** What is the second line of the hymn that begins: "We plough the fields and scatter"?

**9B** Which herb is often used when cooking lamb?

---

**11A** What is the difference between a mountain ash and a rowan tree?

**11B** In what season do daffodils flower?

---

**13A** What is a Granny Smith?

**13B** The foxglove produces a drug called digitalis. What part of the body does it treat?

---

**15A** What type of wood are archers' bows usually made from?

**15B** If someone is said to offer an olive branch, what does this mean?

1A  Yellow.
1B  The koala bear.

---

3A  A type of lettuce.
3B  Snapdragon.

---

5A  Banana.
5B  Honeysuckle.

---

7A  Small pruning shears.
7B  The conker.

---

9A  "The good seed on the land."
9B  Rosemary.

---

11A  They are the same.
11B  Spring.

---

13A  A kind of apple.
13B  The heart.

---

15A  Yew.
15B  They are offering peace.

# Toys & Games

**1A** Which range of soft toys includes characters called Rhinokey and Eleroo?

**1B** At the start of Scrabble, how many letter tiles are picked up by each player?

**3A** Which card game has a name that also means a structure over a gap?

**3B** M.L.P. are the initials of a girl's toy that comes complete with its own hairbrush. What is it?

**5A** In chess, how many squares may a king move in one turn?

**5B** In which game might you say "Have you got Mr Soot the Sweep?

**7A** What soft toy was named after Theodore Roosevelt, President of the USA?

**7B** In which game has Dr Black been found murdered in the cellar?

**9A** Which game has a top score of 180?

**9B** How many sides are there on a pair of dice?

**11A** What is Princess Adora's name when she becomes the Princess of Power?

**11B** In Risk, what is each player aiming to do?

**13A** In which board game do you get given £200 when you pass "Go"?

**13B** Who is He-Man's deadly enemy?

**15A** Which arcade game features a round, gobbling head and ghosts?

**15B** Complete the name of this game: Tic-Tac- . . .

# Toys & Games

**1A** The Wuzzles.
**1B** Seven.

---

**3A** Bridge.
**3B** My Little Pony.

---

**5A** One.
**5B** Happy Families.

---

**7A** The teddy bear.
**7B** Cluedo.

---

**9A** Darts.
**9B** Twelve.

---

**11A** She-Ra.
**11B** Control the world.

---

**13A** Monopoly.
**13B** Skeletor.

---

**15A** Pac-Man.
**15B** Toe.

# Royalty

**1A**  One of the Queen's homes is called Holyrood House. In which city is it?

**1B**  Who called for three fiddlers?

---

**3A**  To whom was Princess Margaret once married?

**3B**  What were the kings of Egypt known as?

---

**5A**  Which sport did Prince Philip take up when he gave up polo?

**5B**  What is the Christian name of the Duchess of Kent?

---

**7A**  Three famous brothers all attended Gordonstoun School. Who are they?

**7B**  For what was Princess Grace of Monaco famous before her marriage?

---

**9A**  Which Princess lives at Thatched House Lodge in Richmond Park?

**9B**  Was Louis XIV of France known as the Sailor King, the Sun King or the Fat King?

---

**11A**  In which European country did Queen Beatrix succeed Queen Juliana?

**11B**  Which English monarch is said to have written "Greensleeves"?

---

**13A**  What relation were Charles II and James II to each other?

**13B**  How many children did Queen Victoria have—four, six or nine?

---

**15A**  Which British monarch abdicated in 1936?

**15B**  In the fairy story by the Brothers Grimm, how many dancing princesses were there?

# Royalty

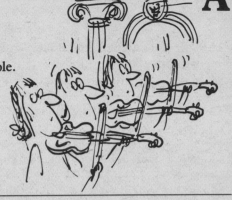

1A  Edinburgh.
1B  Old King Cole.

3A  Lord Snowdon (the Earl of Snowdon, previously Mr Anthony Armstrong-Jones).

3B  Pharaohs.

5A  Carriage driving.

5B  Katharine.

7A  The Prince of Wales, Prince Andrew and Prince Edward.

7B  She was a film star (Grace Kelly).

9A  Princess Alexandra.

9B  The Sun King.

11A  The Netherlands (Holland).

11B  Henry VIII.

13A  They were brothers.

13B  Nine.

15A  Edward VIII (The Duke of Windsor).

15B  Twelve.

# Your Body

1A Which finger is known as the pinkie?

1B Does a hair grow out of a follicle, a manacle or a pinnacle?

---

3A Which part of the body might be aquiline, snub, retroussé or Roman?

3B You might belong to group A, B, AB or O. What does this describe?

---

5A Where on your body is your solar plexus?

5B How long can a human being survive without water? Is it 3 days, 7 days or 13 days?

---

7A Where is your Achilles tendon? ✓

7B Is a shoulder blade a scapula, a patella or an ulna?

---

9A What part of the body does an opthalmologist treat?

9B Why do rugby players wear headbands?

---

11A What can be described as either sensory or motor?

11B Which part of your body might suffer from fallen arches?

---

13A What do you call the regions on either side of the head between the eyebrows and hairline?

13B Which muscle has two auricles and two ventricles?

---

15A What organ is affected by the disease hepatitis? ✓

15B "North and south" is rhyming slang for which part of the body?

# Your Body

1A  The little finger.
1B  A follicle.

3A  The nose.
3B  Your blood type.

5A  Below your ribcage.
5B  Three days.

7A  In your heel.
7B  A scapula.

9A  The eyes.
9B  To protect their ears.

11A  Nerves.
11B  Your feet.

13A  The temples.
13B  The heart.

15A  The liver.
15B  The mouth.

# Plays & Poems

1A  Who wrote the words for the musical *Joseph & the Amazing Technicolor Dreamcoat*?

1B  What was the Christian name of Mr Belloc, who wrote *Cautionary Verses*?

---

3A  Michael Crawford starred on stage as a famous American showman. What was his name?  ✓

3B  Which of these was not a playwright: Sheridan, Chaucer, Pinter, Chekhov?

---

5A  "Season of mists and mellow fruitfulness"—which season was Keats referring to?

5B  Which pantomime character loves and loses Cinderella?

---

7A  What nationality was Hamlet?  ✓

7B  Did the poet Rupert Brooke die in his teens, twenties, thirties or forties?

---

9A  Who wrote the long-running play *The Mousetrap*?

9B  Samuel Taylor Coleridge wrote a poem called "The Ancient . . ."—what?

---

11A  Which play has a fairy called Tinkerbell?

11B  Tennyson wrote: "Come into the garden . . ."—who?

---

13A  Who went to sea with an owl in a pea-green boat?  ✓

13B  Where did Bill Brewer and Peter Gurney—among others—go to on an old grey mare?

---

15A  Who wrote a poem that begins "'Twas brillig, and the slithy toves . . ."?

15B  Which famous musical is based on some poems by T. S. Eliot?

# Plays & Poems

**1A** Tim Rice.
**1B** Hilaire.

**3A** Barnum (Phineas T. Barnum).
**3B** Chaucer.

**5A** Autumn.
**5B** Buttons.

**7A** Danish.
**7B** Twenties.

**9A** Agatha Christie.
**9B** Mariner.

**11A** *Peter Pan*.
**11B** Maud.

**13A** A pussycat.
**13B** Widdicombe Fair.

**15A** Lewis Carroll.
(*The Hunting of the Snark*.)
**15B** *Cats*.

# Wild Life

**1A** Which animal is known as "the ship of the desert"?

**1B** What type of ape lives on the Rock of Gibraltar?

---

**3A** How many arms has a squid? ✓

**3B** Which bird is the symbol of peace?

---

**5A** Cabbage white, peacock and painted lady are all types of—what?

**5B** What is the difference between a coyote and a prairie wolf?

---

**7A** Where is a rattlesnake's rattle? ✓

**7B** Where does a marsupial carry its young?

---

**9A** What type of animal is a mustang?

**9B** A slowworm is not a worm at all. What is it?

---

**11A** Which is the most common British bird?

**11B** An invertebrate is an animal without a—what?

---

**13A** What animal is sometimes referred to as Brock?

**13B** Which animal is known as the king of the beasts?

---

**15A** Which bird is said to be unlucky alone and lucky in pairs?

**15B** An aphid is another name for a—what?

# Wild Life

**1A** The camel.
**1B** Barbary.

---

**3A** Ten.
**3B** The dove.

---

**5A** Butterfly.
**5B** They are the same.

---

**7A** At the tail end of its body.
**7B** In its pouch.

---

**9A** A horse.
**9B** A lizard.

---

**11A** The chaffinch.
**11B** Backbone (spine).

---

**13A** The badger.
**13B** The lion.

---

**15A** A magpie.
**15B** Greenfly.

# Clothes

1A A sou'wester is principally worn by seamen. What is it?

1B Were mini-skirts in fashion in the mid-1950s, '60s, or '70s?

---

3A What name is given to the special clothes worn by monks and nuns?

3B On which part of the body are epaulettes worn? ✓

---

5A Which famous English duke invented a waterproof boot which bears his name?

5B Who might wear a burnoose?

---

7A Which famous husband and wife team designed the Princess of Wales's wedding dress?

7B What type of animal produces the wool called cashmere?

---

9A What type of hat did Charlie Chaplin's "Tramp" wear?

9B Crew, boat, sweetheart and turtle are all types of — what?

---

11A What is or was a winklepicker?

11B For what sport might you wear salopettes?

---

13A What nationality was fashion designer Coco Chanel?

13B Who has been portrayed wearing a long, multi-coloured scarf?

---

15A What do cowboys wear when riding to protect their trousers?

15B Which hard-wearing cotton fabric comes from the French town of Nîmes? ✓

# Clothes

**1A**  A waterproof hat.
**1B**  1960s.

---

**3A**  Habits.
**3B**  The shoulders.

---

**5A**  The Duke of Wellington.
**5B**  An Arab.

---

**7A**  The Emmanuels.
**7B**  A goat.

---

**9A**  A bowler.
**9B**  Neckline.

---

**11A**  A type of shoe.
**11B**  Skiing (they're a kind of dungaree).

---

**13A**  French.
**13B**  Dr Who.

---

**15A**  Chaps.
**15B**  Denim (de Nîmes).

**1A** What is the modern name for a charabanc?

**1B** To go faster, you shout, "mush!" How are you travelling?

---

**3A** In which country were troikas once used?

**3B** Where on an aircraft are the ailerons?

---

**5A** Which film starring Charlton Heston featured a spectacular chariot race?

**5B** Who might own a hearse?

---

**7A** Tennessee Williams wrote a play called *A Streetcar Named* . . . —what?

**7B** A dhow, a ketch, a brig and a gig. Which of these is not a sailing vessel?

---

**9A** What is the British name for the American "station wagon"?

**9B** On a ship, what is the kitchen called?

---

**11A** Who propels a gondola?

**11B** A Boeing 747 is often known as a—what?

---

**13A** Which European city has an underground railway called the Metro?

**13B** How many wheels has a unicycle?

---

**15A** Which Chinese vessel has a name that means "rubbish"?

**15B** Is a drophead coupé a type of pushchair, mail coach, sports car or railway carriage?

**1A** A coach. (A motorcoach, used for outings, etc.)
**1B** By dog-drawn sled.

---

**3A** Russia.
**3B** On the wings.

---

**5A** *Ben Hur*.
**5B** An undertaker.

---

**7A** *Desire*.
**7B** A gig.

---

**9A** Estate car (or shooting brake).
**9B** The galley.

---

**11A** A gondolier.
**11B** Jumbo jet.

---

**13A** Paris.
**13B** One.

---

**15A** A junk.
**15B** Sports car.

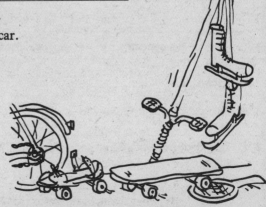

# Arts & Artists

# Q

1A  What kind of paint do artists generally use on canvas?

1B  Which London museum was named after an English queen and her consort?

---

3A  Modern American artist Andy Warhol painted a famous picture of a tin of—what?

3B  Which country is most famous for its fruit and flower paintings?

---

5A  What name is given to a very small painting showing fine detail?

5B  Who was famous for his paintings of Venice? Was it Canneloni, Rigoletto, Canaletto, or Rigatoni?

---

7A  Tenniel illustrated two very famous books. Name one.

7B  What is the Christian name of Thelwell, famous for his pony cartoons?

---

9A  What name is given to a painting done on a wall?

9B  Monet, Pisarro, El Greco and Renoir—which of these was not an Impressionist painter?

---

11A  What nationality was the goldsmith Fabergé, famous for his jewelled Easter eggs?

11B  Frans Hals painted "The Laughing . . ."—what?

---

13A  Is Degas famous for his paintings of flowers, circuses, ballet dancers or sea scenes?

13B  From which country does the Willow Pattern design come?

---

15A  Who created the girls of St Trinians and the boys of St Custards?

15B  Alessandro di Mariano Filipepi painted "The Birth of Venus". By what name is he better known?

# Arts & Artists

1A  Oil.
1B  The Victoria and Albert Museum.

3A  Soup.
3B  Holland.

5A  A miniature.
5B  Canaletto.

7A  *Alice's Adventures in Wonderland* and *Through the Looking-Glass.*
7B  Norman.

9A  A mural.
9B  El Greco.

11A  Russian.
11B  Cavalier.

13A  Ballet dancers.
13B  China.

15A  Ronald Searle.
15B  Botticelli.

# Films

**1A** Superman is unable to see through one substance. What is it?

**1B** In which country was film actor and comedian Bob Hope born?

**3A** In *Star Wars*, what is the name of Han Solo's space ship?

**3B** Which was the first James Bond film ever made?

**5A** From which film does the song "Over the Rainbow" come?

**5B** In Sylvester Stallone's "Rocky" films, what kind of sportsman does he play?

**7A** Which famous pop group made a film called *Help*?

**7B** In the Disney film, what colour is Snow White's hair?

**9A** What was unusual about Yul Brynner's appearance?

**9B** In which country was *The Sound of Music* set?

**11A** In the film *E.T.*, what was E.T. dressed up as, for Hallowe'en?

**11B** Norma Jean Baker was the real name of a film actress who died in 1962. Who was she?

**13A** What does Michael J. Fox stand on to move quickly in *Back to the Future*?

**13B** What child star of the 1930s sang "On the Good Ship Lollipop"?

**15A** How many Ghostbusters are there in the film of that name?

**15B** In the film *Mary Poppins*, what is the occupation of the character played by Dick Van Dyke?

# Films

1A Lead.
1B England.

3A The Millennium Falcon.
3B *Dr No.*

5A *The Wizard of Oz.*
5B A boxer.

7A The Beatles.
7B Black.

9A His bald head.
9B Austria.

11A A ghost.
11B Marilyn Monroe.

13A A skateboard.
13B Shirley Temple.

15A Three.
15B Chimney sweep.

# The Past

**1A** Who came from Normandy in 1066 to fight King Harold?

**1B** What was the slogan of Mrs Pankhurst and her followers?

---

**3A** What was the *Spirit of St. Louis*?

**3B** Was Capability Brown a famous architect, composer, landscape gardener or furniture maker?

---

**5A** Who is said to have asked to be painted exactly as he was, "warts and all"?

**5B** What was the Tin Lizzie?

---

**7A** Which famous ship struck an iceberg on its maiden voyage?

**7A** The favourite drink of the Anglo-Saxons was mead. What is it made of?

---

**9A** Who was the general who invaded Britain in 55 BC?

**9B** What was the occupation of Sir Henry Irving?

---

**11A** Which London station is named after a great battle?

**11B** In AD 79, Pompeii was smothered in ash and lava —from which volcano?

---

**13A** Who travelled over the sea to Skye with Flora Macdonald?

**13B** If you were locked in a pillory, would you be held by your ankles, your wrists, your neck and ankles, or your neck and wrists?

---

**15A** What happened to the Crystal Palace in 1936?

**15B** The tomb of which boy pharaoh was discovered by Howard Carter and Lord Caernarvon in 1922?

# The Past

**1A** William the Conqueror.

**1B** Votes for Women.

---

**3A** An aeroplane (in which Charles Lindbergh made the first solo non-stop Atlantic flight).

**3B** Landscape gardener.

---

**5A** Oliver Cromwell.

**5B** A car. (The Model-T Ford.)

---

**7A** The *SS Titanic*.

**7B** Honey.

---

**9A** Julius Caesar.

**9B** He was an actor.

---

**11A** Waterloo.

**11B** Vesuvius.

---

**13A** Bonnie Prince Charlie.

**13B** Your neck and wrists.

---

**15A** It was burnt to the ground.

**15B** Tutankhamun.

# Songs & Music

**1A** Barry Manilow sings a song about events in a nightclub called—what?

**1B** Which famous composer had the Christian name Ludwig? ✓

---

**3A** Traditional Jazz music originated in the Deep South —of which country?

**3B** Which of these instruments can produce the highest note: oboe, clarinet, flute, piccolo? ✓

---

**5A** Complete the first line of this old song? "There was I, waiting at the . . ."—what?

**5B** Does *legato* mean smoothly, majestically, very loudly or brightly?

---

**7A** Sailors used to sing special songs to help them work. What were they called?

**7B** Which musical includes a song called "I Feel Pretty"?

---

**9A** Was Johann Strauss known as The Prince of Jazz, the Waltz King or the Duke of Swing?

**9B** Where might you sing "You'll Never Walk Alone"?

---

**11A** Was the songwriter Irving Berlin born in 1888, 1915, 1933 or 1947?

**11B** How many strings has a guitar?

---

**13A** What type of music is the composer Giuseppe Verdi most famous for?

**13B** In the old song, a nightingale sang in a well-known London square. Which one?

---

**15A** Which instrument has a U-shaped section that slides in and out?

**15B** Which famous singer was known as The Old Groaner?

# Songs & Music

**1A** The Copacabana.
**1B** Beethoven.

---

**3A** The USA.
**3B** Piccolo.

---

**5A** Church.
**5B** Smoothly.

---

**7A** Sea shanties.
**7B** *West Side Story*.

---

**9A** The Waltz King.
**9B** At a football match.

---

**11A** 1888.
**11B** Six.

---

**13A** Opera.
**13B** Berkeley.

---

**15A** Trombone.
**15B** Bing Crosby.

# Pot Luck

1A What is the name of the principal London airport?

1B Quakers—are they a sort of cereal, frightened people, or a religious sect?

3A With what weapon did David kill Goliath?

3B In which nursery rhyme does a small dog see something that makes him laugh?

5A Which day of the week is a holy day for Moslems?

5B The French word for pigskin is used to describe fine china. What is this word? ✓

7A What do the initials OHMS stand for?

7B A wooden cylinder filled with graphite—what does this describe? ✓

9A What is rubella better known as?

9B Complete this proverb: Once bitten . . .

11A What do the initials s.a.e. stand for?

11B Oriental means "eastern". What's another word for western? ✓

13A What was the hobby of Agatha Christie's Miss Marple?

13B Which flower is used as a symbol of remembrance by the Royal British Legion?

15A Where are the Promenade Concerts held?

15B In what sort of room might you see a recorder, a QC, an usher and a plaintiff?

# Pot Luck

1A  Heathrow.
1B  A religious sect.

3A  A sling.
3B  *Hey Diddle Diddle*.

5A  Friday.
5B  Porcelain.

7A  On Her Majesty's Service.
7B  A pencil.

9A  German measles.
9B  Twice shy.

11A  Stamped addressed envelope.
11B  Occidental.

13A  Detecting crime.
13B  The poppy.

15A  The Albert Hall.
15B  A courtroom.

HOW TRIVIAL CAN YOU GET?

HOW TRIVIAL CAN YOU GET?

# Can You Name Them?

**1A** The girl in *Peter Pan*.
**1B** The king who burnt the cakes.

**3A** The red-nosed reindeer.
**3B** The saint who slew a dragon.

**5A** The brother of the apostle James.
**5B** The eldest of Louisa M. Alcott's "Little Women".

**7A** The piper's son who stole a pig.
**7B** The wife of Ronald Reagan.

**9A** The wife of King George VI.
**9B** The girl who put a kettle on.

**11A** The sister of Donald Duck.
**11B** The last king of France.

**13A** The postman with a black-and-white cat.
**13B** The Brönte sister who wrote *Jane Eyre*.

**15A** The girl in *The Wizard of Oz*.
**15B** The first man.

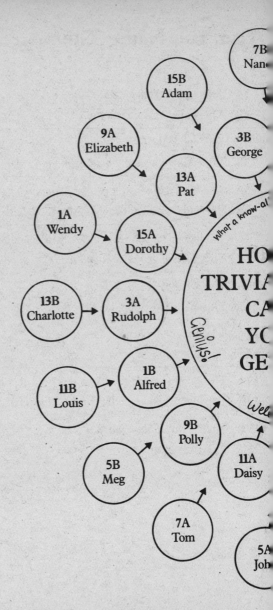

7B
Nan⋅

15B
Adam

9A
Elizabeth

3B
George

13A
Pat

1A
Wendy

15A
Dorothy

13B
Charlotte

3A
Rudolph

1B
Alfred

11B
Louis

9B
Polly

5B
Meg

11A
Daisy

7A
Tom

5A
Joh⋅

What a know-all

Genius!

Wel⋅

HO
TRIVI
CA
YO
GE

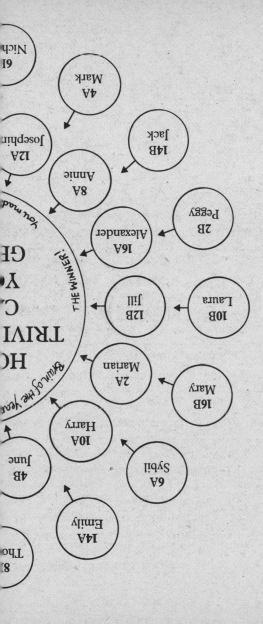

# Can You Name Them?

2A  Robin Hood's girlfriend.
2B  The chalet maid in Hi-De-Hi.

4A  Margaret Thatcher's son.
4B  Terry Scott's TV wife.

6A  Mrs Fawlty of Fawlty Towers.
6B  The saint known as "Santa Claus".

8A  The little dressmaker's "Rag Dolly" friend.
8B  The blue Tank Engine.

10A  Prince Charles's second son.
10B  Jean's little girl in *Our Backyard*.

12A  Napoleon's wife.
12B  She tumbled after Jack.

14A  The owner of Bagpuss.
14B  The notorious "Ripper".

16A  The great king, whose horse was Bucephalus.
16B  She has a garden of bells, shells and maids.

# Pot Luck

**2A** Dartmouth.

**2B** St Valentine's.

**4A** In the docks.

**4B** Catgut.

**6A** Leofric.

**6B** Lace.

**8A** Spain (España).

**8B** A skull and crossbones.

**10A** Photography.

**10B** A type of knot.

**12A** On the moon.

**12B** In an aeroplane.

**14A** *Sing a Song of Sixpence*.

**14B** The Victoria Cross.

**16A** Count with it.

**16B** Trades Union Congress.

# Pot Luck

**2A** Army officers train at Sandhurst. Where do naval officers train?

**2B** What saint's day occurs on February 14th?

---

**4A** Where would you find a stevedore working?

**4B** What were the strings of early violins made of?

---

**6A** Was Lady Godiva married to Leofric, Baldric, Tostag or Red Robert?

**6B** Nottingham is famous for the manufacture of a certain fine fabric. Which one?

---

**8A** If a car has the letter 'E' on the back, what country does it come from?

**8B** What does the Jolly Roger, or pirates' flag, depict?

---

**10A** If you were interested in viewfinders, shutter speeds and ASA numbers, what would your hobby be?

**10B** What is a sheepshank?

---

**12A** Where is the Sea of Tranquillity?

**12B** Louis Blériot was the first person to cross the English Channel in a certain way. How?

---

**14A** In which nursery rhyme is a royal person eating honey and bread?

**14B** What medal bears the inscription "For Valour"?

---

**16A** If you had an abacus, would you play it, cook it, dig it up or count with it?

**16B** What do the initials TUC stand for?

# Songs & Music

**2A** The Beatles.
**2B** Four.

---

**4A** Milan.
**4B** A piano.

---

**6A** Dublin.
**6B** "The Star-Spangled Banner."

---

**8A** Handel.
**8B** E.

---

**10A** Frank Sinatra.
**10B** The trumpet.

---

**12A** Mozart.
**12B** *Oliver!*

---

**14A** Hat.
**14B** Tulips.

---

**16A** A sousaphone.
**16B** "Auld Lang Syne."

# Songs & Music

**2A** Which group first sang about a yellow submarine?

**2B** How many singers are needed to perform barbershop harmony?

**4A** Is the La Scala Opera House in Rome, Milan, Brazil or Vienna?

**4B** On what musical instrument might you see the name Steinway?

**6A** Which city is mentioned in the song "Cockles and Mussels"?

**6B** What is the American national anthem known as?

**8A** Which famous composer had the first names George Frideric?

**8B** The basic notes on a violin are G, D, A and one other. What is it?

**10A** Which famous American singer is known as Ol' Blue Eyes?

**10B** What instrument did Louis Armstrong play?

**12A** Which great composer was the subject of the film *Amadeus*?

**12B** In which musical does an orphan boy sing "Where Is Love"?

**14A** Complete the first line of this old song: "Where did you get that . . ."—what?

**14B** There's a well-known old song called "Tiptoe through the . . ."—what?

**16A** Which is the largest, a tuba, a French horn, a sousaphone or a euphonium?

**16B** An old Scottish song is traditionally sung on New Year's Eve. What is it called?

# The Past

**2A** Wireless.

**2B** The *Bounty*.

---

**4A** The Great Fire of London.

**4B** Boudicca (Boadicea).

---

**6A** The spider.

**6B** Methuselah.

---

**8A** Italian.

**8B** World War I.

---

**10A** Stonehenge.

**10B** North America.

---

**12A** Nero.

**12B** Twelve.

---

**14A** The Gestapo.

**14B** Queen Victoria's.

---

**16A** The plague.

**16B** One eye and one arm.

# The Past

2A  What is the old-fashioned word for a radio?

2B  Aboard which ship did Fletcher Christian lead a mutiny?

4A  Which disaster of 1666 does the Monument commemorate?

4B  Who was queen of the Iceni tribe who defeated the Romans?

6A  Which creature is associated with Robert the Bruce?

6B  In the Bible, who lived over 900 years?

8A  What nationality was Leonardo da Vinci?

8B  In which war was the Battle of the Somme fought?

10A  Which ancient monument stands on Salisbury Plain?

10B  In 1620 the Pilgrim Fathers set sail in the *Mayflower*. Where to?

12A  Which Roman emperor is said to have fiddled while Rome burned?

12B  In old currency, how many pence was one shilling worth?

14A  Was the German secret state police force in the days of the Nazis called – the SS, the Gestapo or the Luftwaffe?

14B  In whose reign were postage stamps first used?

16A  What disease, which killed countless people in the Middle Ages, was known as the Black Death?

16B  Did Nelson lose one arm and one leg, two arms, one eye and one arm or one eye and one leg?

# Films

**2A** David Bowie.
**2B** John Wayne.

**4A** Dumbo.
**4B** *Butch Cassidy and the Sundance Kid.*

**6A** Oscars.
**6B** Judy Garland.

**8A** Steven Spielberg.
**8B** *Gone with the Wind.*

**10A** Short Round.
**10B** Tarzan.

**12A** Peter Sellers.
**12B** Stanley (Stan).

**14A** A car.
**14B** Meryl Streep.

**16A** Extra Terrestrial.
**16B** Clint Eastwood.

# Films

**2A**  Which singer/actor starred in the film *The Man Who Fell to Earth*?

**2B**  Marion Michael Morrison was a famous western star. By what name was he better known?

**4A**  Which elephant had ears so big he could fly?

**4B**  In which film did two actors leap into a river holding hands?

**6A**  By what name are the American Film Academy awards usually known?

**6B**  Actress and singer Liza Minnelli had a famous mother. Who was she?

**8A**  Who directed *Close Encounters of the Third Kind*?

**8B**  In which film does Rhett Butler say, "Frankly, my dear, I don't give a damn."?

**10A**  In the film *Indiana Jones and the Temple of Doom*, what was the name of Indy's boy companion?

**10B**  Whom did Johnny Weissmuller first portray on film?

**12A**  In the *Pink Panther* films, who played Inspector Clouseau?

**12B**  What was the Christian name of Ollie Hardy's partner Laurel?

**14A**  In the film of that name, what was Chitty Chitty Bang Bang?

**14B**  Which famous film actress's name is an anagram of MERLY PETERS?

**16A**  In the film of that name, what do the initials ET stand for?

**16B**  Who starred in the film *A Fistful of Dollars*?

# Art & Artists

2A  Mosaic.
2B  Edward Lear.

---

4A  Cartoons.
4B  Because he was painting the ceiling.

---

6A  He had very short legs.
6B  Horses.

---

8A  They all are, or were, sculptors.
8B  Dutch.

---

10A  Henry VIII. (The bride was Anne of Cleves.)
10B  Red.

---

12A  Still life.
12B  2H.

---

14A  Paris.
14B  The Battle of Hastings.

---

16A  The Haywain.
16B  Pablo.

# Art & Artists

**2A** What name is given to a design made up of small pieces of coloured glass or stone?

**2B** Who illustrated Edward Lear's limericks?

**4A** What form of art are Giles, Mac, Trog and Graham famous for?

**4B** When decorating the Sistine chapel in Rome, Michelangelo had to lie on his back. Why?

**6A** What was unusual about the appearance of the French artist Toulouse-Lautrec?

**6B** Which animals would you expect to see in a painting by George Stubbs?

**8A** Hepworth, Epstein, Rodin and Moore—what do these names have in common?

**8B** What nationality was Rembrandt?

**10A** Who selected a bride from a flattering portrait of her by Hans Holbein?

**10B** What colour is the pigment called madder?

**12A** What name is given to a painting of objects on a table?

**12B** Which of these pencils is the hardest: B, HB, 2H or 4B?

**14A** In which city is the Louvre Museum?

**14B** Does the Bayeaux Tapestry tell the story of the Battle of Hastings, the Fall of the Roman Empire or the Crimean War?

**16A** Which famous painting by Constable shows a wagon in a stream?

**16B** What was Picasso's Christian name?

# Transport

**2A**  Concorde.
**2B**  An early type of bicycle.

---

**4A**  It has a fold-down hood or removal roof.
**4B**  Galley.

---

**6A**  One.
**6B**  Perambulator.

---

**8A**  On an elephant.
**8B**  San Francisco.

---

**10A**  Two.
**10B**  A porthole.

---

**12A**  Motorcycle.
**12B**  A sedan.

---

**14A**  A mooring rope.
**14B**  The Spitfire.

---

**16A**  A surrey.
**16B**  Prisoners. (It's a police van.)

# Transport

**2A** Which airliner has a machmeter in the cabin?

**2B** What was a "boneshaker"?

---

**4A** What is special about a car known as a "convertible".

**4B** Biremes, triremes and quinqueremes were all types of—what?

---

**6A** How many people can ride in or on a sulky?

**6B** What is the word "pram" short for?

---

**8A** If you were in a howdah, how would you be travelling?

**8B** Which American city is famous for its cable cars?

---

**10A** How many wheels has a rickshaw?

**10B** What is a small round window on the side of a ship's hull called?

---

**12A** Norton, Kawasaki and Honda are or were all makes of—what?

**12B** What name was given to a closed chair, carried on poles by two bearers?

---

**14A** In boating terms, what is a painter?

**14B** What was the main type of fighter aircraft used in the Battle of Britain?

---

**16A** In the musical *Oklahoma*, what type of vehicle has "a fringe on top"?

**16B** Who or what are transported in a Black Maria?

# Clothes

2A  Your elbows.
2B  Round your waist.

4A  Panty-hose.
4B  In a tie.

6A  Hat.
6B  A kimono.

8A  A ballerina.
8B  Cardigan.

10A  The New Look.
10B  A sporran.

12A  A glove.
12B  Crinolines.

14A  A wet suit.
14B  Sleeves.

16A  Shoe.
16B  A deer-stalker.

# Clothes

**2A** When skateboarding, you should wear protectors on your head, your knees and—what else?

**2B** Where would you wear a cummerbund?

**4A** What do Americans call tights?

**4B** Where would you see a Windsor knot?

**6A** Homburg, trilby and boater are all types of—what?

**6B** What is the robe traditionally worn by a Japanese woman called?

**8A** Who might wear a tutu?

**8B** What knitted garment was named after a 19th century earl?

**10A** In 1947 did Christian Dior invent the New Style, the New Fashion, or the New Look?

**10B** What is the name of the fur-covered pouch a Scotsman wears with his kilt?

**12A** Is a gauntlet a type of sock, a glove or a small scarf?

**12B** What did Victorian women wear to make their skirts stand out?

**14A** If you were skin-diving in cold waters, what might you wear to keep warm?

**14B** What might be described as dolman, raglan or leg-o'-mutton?

**16A** Court, sling-back, platform and brogue. These are all types of—what?

**16B** What kind of hat did Sherlock Holmes wear?

# Wild Life

**2A**  A bird.
**2B**  The squirrel's.

---

**4A**  Giraffe.
**4B**  Cattle.

---

**6A**  A boar.
**6B**  Eight.

---

**8A**  A goldcrest.
**8B**  One.

---

**10A**  The elephant.
**10B**  A pearl.

---

**12A**  The chameleon.
**12B**  Shells.

---

**14A**  The silkworm.
**14B**  Orang-utan.

---

**16A**  A drone.
**16B**  Ravens.

# Wild Life

**2A** What kind of creature is a chiff-chaff?

**2B** Which animal's home is called a drey?

---

**4A** Camelopard is the old name for a—what?

**4B** Jersey and Friesian are breeds of which animal?

---

**6A** What is a male pig called?

**6B** How many legs has a spider?

---

**8A** What is the smallest British bird? Is it a goldcrest, a sparrow, a wren or a bluetit?

**8B** How many humps has a dromedary?

---

**10A** Which animal is Hannibal supposed to have used when crossing the Alps?

**10B** What precious object grows inside an oyster?

---

**12A** Which reptile changes colour to blend with its surroundings?

**12B** What does a conchologist study?

---

**14A** What feeds only on the leaves of the mulberry tree?

**14B** Which reddish ape has a name which is Malay for "Man of the Forest"?

---

**16A** What is a male bee called?

**16B** Which birds make their home in the Tower of London?

# Plays & Poems

**2A** Robert Burns.
**2B** Comedies.

**4A** "The boy stood on the burning deck."
**4B** *Aladdin*.

**6A** *Hiawatha* (by Longfellow).
**6B** Solomon Grundy.

**8A** All the characters wear roller skates.
**8B** Tolstoy.

**10A** Norwegian.
**10B** Elaine Paige.

**12A** He enticed away their children.
**12B** William Shakespeare's.

**14A** *Light Brigade*.
**14B** Toby.

**16A** *My Fair Lady*.
**16B** Wales.

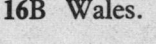

# Plays & Poems

**2A** Which famous Scottish poet wrote *Tam O'Shanter* and *Comin' Through the Rye*?

**2B** Is the dramatist Alan Ayckbourn famous for his comedies, tragedies or musicals?

**4A** "Whence all but he had fled" is the second line of a famous poem. What's the first line?

**4B** Which pantomime has a character called Widow Twankey?

**6A** In which poem does Minnehaha appear?

**6B** Who was "born on Monday, christened on Tuesday, married on Wednesday . . ."?

**8A** What's unusual about the musical *Starlight Express?*

**8B** Which of these was not a poet: Sassoon, Shelley, Milton, Tolstoy?

**10A** Was the playwright Henrik Ibsen Dutch, German, Swedish or Norwegian?

**10B** Who first played the part of Evita in the musical of that name?

**12A** In Robert Browning's poem, what was the Pied Piper's revenge on the people of Hamelin?

**12B** Whose plays are performed at Stratford-on-Avon?

**14A** Tennyson wrote a poem called *The Charge of the* . . ."—what?

**14B** In Punch and Judy, what is Punch's dog called? ✓

**16A** George Bernard Shaw's play *Pygmalion* became a famous musical. What was its title?

**16B** Of which country was Dylan Thomas writing in his poem *Under Milk Wood*?

# Your Body

**2A** A vampire.

**2B** Your larynx.

---

**4A** Fingerprints.

**4B** The feet.

---

**6A** A black eye.

**6B** On the head. (It's a soft gap between the bones of the skull.)

---

**8A** Your jaw.

**8B** Cold.

---

**10A** The kidneys.

**10B** Your brain.

---

**12A** On the eyes.

**12B** At the base of your finger- and toe-nails.

---

**14A** The calf.

**14B** Touch.

---

**16A** The lungs.

**16B** The femur.

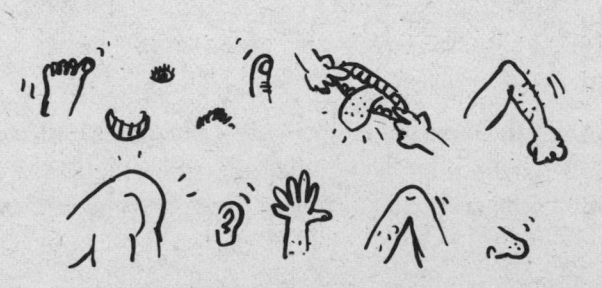

# Your Body

**2A** What type of evil being is supposed to have extra-long canines?

**2B** Is your Adam's apple your larynx, pharynx or appendix?

**4A** What are identified by loops, whorls and arches?

**4B** Which part of the body does a chiropodist care for?

**6A** What injury was supposed to be relieved by applying a piece of steak?

**6B** Where on a baby would you find the fontanelle?

**8A** What is formed by your upper and lower mandibles?

**8B** If you were suffering from hypothermia, would you be cold, thirsty, insane or shortsighted?

**10A** Which organs clean the blood?

**10B** If someone refers to your "grey cells", what are they talking about?

**12A** Where can cataracts sometimes form?

**12B** Where on your body are your half-moons?

**14A** What part of the body has the same name as a young farm animal?

**14B** The five senses are taste, smell, sight, hearing and—what?

**16A** Which part of the body does pneumonia affect?

**16B** Is the thigh bone called the tibia, the fibula or the femur?

# Royalty

2A  Balloons.

2B  Two (Anne Boleyn
and Katherine Howard).

4A  1900.

4B  Oberon.

6A  Windsor.

6B  Hans Andersen.

8A  France.

8B  George III.

10A  The Emperor of Japan.

10B  Mrs Mark Phillips.

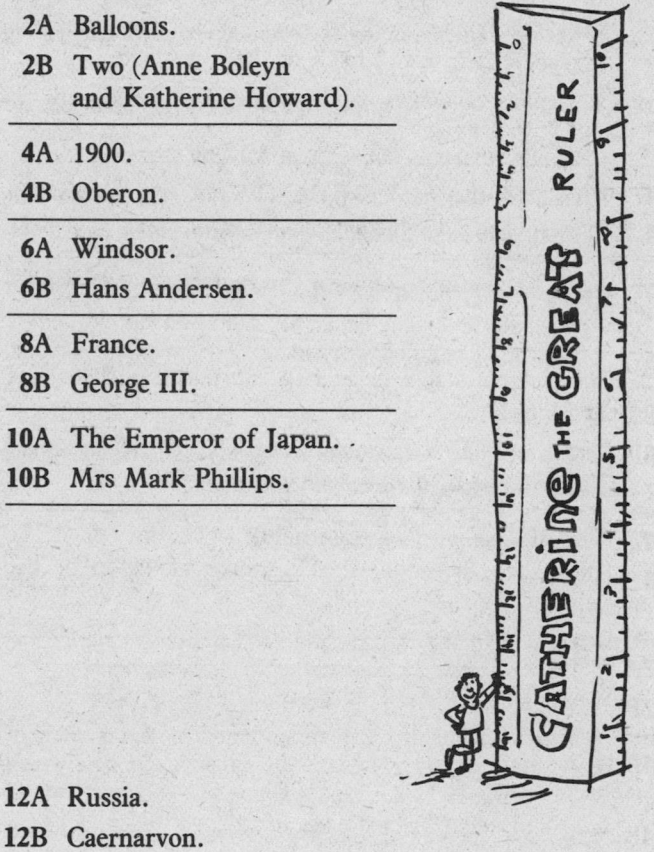

12A  Russia.

12B  Caernarvon.

14A  The Queen of Hearts in *Alice in Wonderland*.

14B  Danish.

16A  She is in residence.

16B  Richard I (the Lionheart).

# Royalty

**2A** When the Prince and Princess of Wales were married, what were tied to the back of their carriage?

**2B** How many of Henry VIII's wives were beheaded?

**4A** In which year was the Queen Mother born?

**4B** What was the name of the King of the Fairies in Shakespeare's *A Midsummer Night's Dream*?

**6A** What is the family name of the British Royal Family?

**6B** Who wrote about an Emperor who had no clothes?

**8A** In which country was the heir to the throne known as the Dauphin?

**8B** British monarch, grandson of George II, married Charlotte, went mad—who was he?

**10A** Who sits on the Chrysanthemum Throne? Is it the Kabaka of Buganda, the Emperor of Japan or the Sultan of Borneo?

**10B** What is Princess Anne's married name?

**12A** Which country did Catherine the Great rule?

**12B** In which castle did the investiture of the Prince of Wales take place?

**14A** Who shouted "Off with his head"?

**14B** What nationality is the Duchess of Gloucester?

**16A** If the Queen's standard is flying over a royal palace, what does it mean?

**16B** Which English king was known as "Coeur de Lion"?

# Toys & Games

**2A**  Round.
**2B**  Donkey Kong.

**4A**  Tiddlywinks.
**4B**  Pursuit.

**6A**  Draughts.
**6B**  Ken.

**8A**  Two.
**8B**  Rainbow Brite.

**10A**  Bingo.
**10B**  Transformers.

**12A**  China.
**12B**  The Holograms.

**14A**  Ludo.
**14B**  The Get Along Gang.

**16A**  The Knave.
**16B**  The Care Bears.

# Toys & Games

# Q

**2A** In Sorry! what shape are the cards?

**2B** Which arcade game features a big ape, ladders and rolling barrels?

**4A** In which game do players try to flick plastic counters into a cup?

**4B** One of the most popular quiz games ever is Trivial—what?

**6A** In which game might you say "I huff you!"?

**6B** Who is Barbie's boyfriend?

**8A** How many players can play Connect 4?

**8B** Which doll has a horse called Starlite and brings colour to anything sad?

**10A** In which game might you hear someone shout "Legs Eleven!"?

**10B** Which range of toys features Heroic Autobots and Evil Decepticons?

**12A** Which country does the game Mah-jong come from?

**12B** To what pop group does the fashion doll Jem belong?

**14A** Its name is Latin for "I play". It's a famous old board game with counters and a dice. What is it?

**14B** To which gang do Dotty Dog and Woolma Lamb belong?

**16A** In a pack of cards, what other name is sometimes given to the Jack?

**16B** Which cuddly bears had their own full-length movie?

# Plants

2A  Buzy Lizzie.
2B  Grapes.

---

4A  Holland.
4B  White.

---

6A  Dandelion (*dent de lion*).
6B  Yam.

---

8A  The dock leaf.
8B  Raspberries.

---

10A  Chelsea.
10B  Mistletoe.

---

12A  Horticulture.
12B  An oak tree.

---

14A  Roses.
14B  Hops.

---

16A  Thyme.
16B  Stifle.

# Plants

**2A** Is the plant *impatiens* also known as Busy Lizzie, Creeping Jenny, Wandering Jew or Poor Man's Orchid?

**2B** What fruit is grown in a vineyard?

**4A** Which country is famous for its bulb fields?

**4B** What colour is a clove of garlic?

**6A** Which flower's name means "lion's tooth"?

**6B** What is another name for a sweet potato?

**8A** Which leaf is supposed to relieve nettle stings?

**8B** What garden fruit grows on "canes"?

**10A** Where in London is a big flower show held every year?

**10B** It has white berries, grows as a parasite on various trees and is used as a Christmas decoration. What is it?

**12A** The science of cultivating land is called agriculture. What is the science of gardening called?

**12B** In what kind of tree did Charles I hide after the Battle of Worcester?

**14A** A comfortable situation is said to be a "bed of . . ."—what?

**14B** What kind of crop is dried in an oast house?

**16A** The most common stuffings you can buy are sage and onion, and parsley and—what?

**16B** Corolla, calyx, stamen, stifle—which of these is not a part of a flower?

# People

2A  Sir Richard Attenborough.
2B  Nepal.

4A  His long hair.
4B  Grantham (Lincolnshire).

6A  As a ballet dancer.
6B  Polish.

8A  Ringo Starr.
8B  Chicago.

10A  Live Aid.
10B  The Queen.

12A  They were father and son.
12B  He was an actor.

14A  Helen of Troy's.
14B  Vincent Van Gogh.

16A  They are both played
by Barry Humphries.
16B  Sitting Bull.

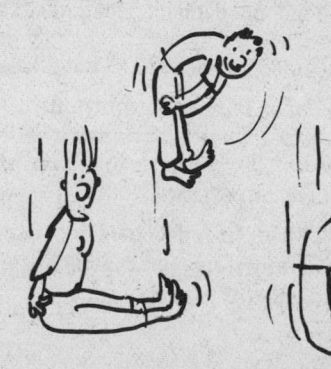

# People

**2A** Sir David Attenborough has an equally famous film producer brother. What is his name?

**2B** Which country do Gurkhas come from? Nepal, Burma or China?

**4A** In the Bible, what was the source of Samson's strength?

**4B** In which town was Margaret Thatcher born?

**6A** How did Dame Margot Fonteyn achieve fame?

**6B** What is the nationality of Pope John Paul II?

**8A** By what name is Richard Starkey better known?

**8B** Al Capone was a notorious American gangster. In which city did he live?

**10A** What was the name of the huge concert organised by Bob Geldof to help the starving people of Ethiopia?

**10B** Who owns all the swans on the River Thames?

**12A** How were land- and water-speed record-holders Malcolm and Donald Campbell related?

**12B** What did Ronald Reagan do before entering politics?

**14A** Whose face is said to have launched a thousand ships?

**14B** Which famous painter cut off his ear?

**16A** What do Dame Edna Everage and Sir Les Patterson have in common?

**16B** Who defeated General Custer at the Battle of Little Big Horn?

# Numbers

2A Four.
2B Five.

---

4A Five.
4B Sixty.

---

6A Thirteen.
6B Three.

---

8A Four.
8B Nine.

---

10A Ten.
10B One.

---

12A 200.
12B Twice.

---

14A Two. (Three went on the expedition, but one remained in the command module.)
14B Every two years.

---

16A Six.
16B Five.

# Numbers

**2A** How many leaves are there on a lucky clover?

**2B** Approximately how many litres of blood are there in the human body—three, five or nine?

**4A** How many rings are there on the Olympic flag?

**4B** If a couple celebrate their diamond wedding, how many years have they been married?

**6A** How many in a "baker's dozen"?

**6B** In the New Testament, how many times did St Peter deny Christ?

**8A** How many stomachs has a cow?

**8B** In the University Boat Race, how many people are there in each boat?

**10A** How many events make up a decathlon?

**10B** Cyclops was remarkable for having how many eyes?

**12A** How many bones are there in the human body, 350, 200, or 180?

**12B** How many times did Richard Burton and Elizabeth Taylor marry?

**14A** How many astronauts travelled in the first spacecraft to land on the moon?

**14B** If an event occurs biennially, how often does it take place?

**16A** How many sides has a hexagon?

**16B** How many men's singles titles did Bjorn Borg take at Wimbledon?

# Science

**2A** The force of an earthquake.
**2B** Brass.

**4A** A beetle.
**4B** Mauve or purple.

**6A** They're the same.
**6B** Light.

**8A** Seventy-six.
**8B** Salt.

**10A** Transac.
**10B** 24-carat.

**12A** Mercury.
**12B** White.

**14A** Sulphur dioxide.
**14B** Another diamond.

**16A** The ear.
**16B** Because they're outside the pull of gravity.

# Science

# Q

**2A** Is the Richter scale used to measure the swing of a pendulum, the force of an earthquake or the acid content of rain?

**2B** What name is given to an alloy of copper and zinc?

---

**4A** A potato can be attacked by a Colorado. What is it?

**4B** What colour is an amethyst?

---

**6A** What's the difference between a meteorite and a shooting star?

**6B** An object which is photosensitive reacts to—what?

---

**8A** How often does Halley's comet appear? Is it every twenty-three, forty-five or seventy-six years?

**8B** What would you put with water to make a saline solution?

---

**10A** Basic, Pascal, Cobol, Transac and Fortran—which of these is not a computer language?

**10B** Pure gold—is it 18-carat, 24-carat or 32-carat?

---

**12A** Which liquid metal used to be called quicksilver?

**12B** Is a magnesium flame white, blue, green or orange?

---

**14A** What makes a "bad egg" smell? Is it hydrous oxide, copper sulphate or sulphur dioxide?

**14B** A diamond is the hardest substance in the world, and can only be cut by one thing. What is it?

---

**16A** What part of the body contains the hammer, anvil and stirrup bones?

**16B** Why are people in space weightless?

# Books

**2A** Greyfriars.
**2B** Anne.

---

**4A** E. Nesbit.
**4B** The *Black Stallion* series.

---

**6A** Moldy Warp.
**6B** Count Dracula.

---

**8A** Narnia.
**8B** Adrian Mole.

---

**10A** A pig.
**10B** School stories.

---

**12A** *Charlie and the Chocolate Factory*.
**12B** Long John Silver.

---

**14A** Tristan.
**14B** Wimbledon Common.

---

**16A** HRH the Prince of Wales.
**16B** He's a detective.

# Books

**Q**

**2A**  What school did Billy Bunter go to?

**2B**  In the books by L.M. Montgomery, who lived in a house called "Green Gables"?

**4A**  Who wrote *The Railway Children*?

**4B**  What famous series of books is written by Walter Farley?

**6A**  In Alison Uttley's *Little Grey Rabbit* books, what is the mole called?

**6B**  What famous character came from Transylvania?

**8A**  What is the name of the mythical country in *The Lion, the Witch and the Wardrobe*?

**8B**  Sue Townsend has written books about a teenage boy. What is his name?

**10A**  In *Alice in Wonderland*, into which animal does the Duchess's baby turn?

**10B**  What kind of stories did Angela Brazil write?

**12A**  On which book was the film about Willie Wonka based?

**12B**  Which character in *Treasure Island* has a wooden leg?

**14A**  In the James Herriot books, what is the name of Siegfried's brother?

**14B**  Where do the Wombles live?

**16A**  Who wrote *The Old Man of Lochnagar*?

**16B**  In the Hardy Boys books, what is the occupation of Frank and Joe's father?

# The World

**2A** Cornwall.

**2B** They are all North American Indians.

---

**4A** Australia.

**4B** Chinese.

---

**6A** The Mediterranean.

**6B** Idi.

---

**8A** Israel.

**8B** Mexico.

---

**10A** Greece.

**10B** They are all deserts.

---

**12A** Texas.

**12B** Norway.

---

**14A** Japan.

**14B** Uncle Sam.

---

**16A** The shamrock.

**16B** Istanbul.

# The World

**2A** In which English county is Bodmin Moor?

**2B** What do Chicksaws, Seminoles and Choctaws have in common?

**4A** In which country is the town called Alice Springs?

**4B** English, Chinese or Spanish—which of these languages is spoken by the greatest number of people?

**6A** In which sea is the island of Malta?

**6B** What was the first name of General Amin, one-time ruler of Uganda?

**8A** Tel Aviv is the largest city of a Middle Eastern country. Which one?

**8B** Which country do tortillas, tacos and guacamole come from?

**10A** In which country were the first modern Olympic games held?

**10B** What do the Kalahari, the Mohave and the Gobi have in common?

**12A** In the USA, which is the "Lone Star" state?

**12B** Which Scandinavian country sends the giant Christmas tree put up in Trafalgar Square each year?

**14A** In which country is Mount Fuji?

**14B** If John Bull symbolizes Britain, who symbolizes the United States—is it Old Smokey, Uncle Sam or Mother Courage?

**16A** What is the national emblem of Ireland?

**16B** What is the modern name for the old city of Constantinople—is it Istanbul, Ahmedabad or Cairo?

# Sport

**2A** Polo.
**2B** No score.

**4A** Lester Piggott.
**4B** Anfield.

**6A** Marylebone Cricket Club.
**6B** Motor racing.

**8A** Eric Bristow.
**8B** Epsom.

**10A** Cricket.
**10B** Ice hockey.

**12A** Charlton.
**12B** Four.

**14A** Lacrosse.
**14B** Cycling.

**16A** Big Daddy.
**16B** Wembley Stadium.

# Sport

**2A** Which game is played by people on horseback, using mallets?

**2B** In tennis, what does the word "love" indicate?

**4A** Which top jockey retired from racing in 1985?

**4B** What is the name of Liverpool FC's ground?

**6A** Which cricket club is known by the initials MCC?

**6B** With what sport is the name Nelson Piquet associated?

**8A** Which darts player is known as "The Crafty Cockney"?

**8B** Where is the race called the Derby run?

**10A** Long on, LBW and a googly. With which sport are these terms connected?

**10B** In which sport is a puck used instead of a ball?

**12A** Two brothers, Bobby and Jack, played in England's winning World Cup soccer team in 1966? What is their surname?

**12B** How often are the Olympic Games held? Is it every 4, 6 or 8 years?

**14A** Which sport was invented by American Indians?

**14B** The Tour de France is a sporting event which takes place every year in France. What sport is involved?

**16A** Shirley Crabtree is a famous wrestler. By what name is he better known?

**16B** Where is the FA Cup Final usually played?

# Words

**A**

**2A** A monologue (or soliloquy).
**2B** Dustman.

---

**4A** Africa.
**4B** He or she has the same name as you.

---

**6A** Noon. (A palindrome reads the same forwards or backwards.)
**6B** Unicorn.

---

**8A** Izquay.
**8B** Oxen.

---

**10A** Wordsworth.
**10B** A dictionary.

---

**12A** The moon.
**12B** Edible.

---

**14A** Marzipan.
**14B** English.

---

**16A** Burn.
**16B** House.

# Words

# Q

**2A** When two people talk, it's a dialogue. What is a speech by one person?

**2B** What is the ordinary name for a refuse collector?

**4A** In which continent is Swahili spoken?

**4B** What does it mean if someone is your namesake?

**6A** Which of these is a palindrome: Lulu, noon, rhythm or unto?

**6B** What mythical beast has a name that means "one horn"?

**8A** How would you say "quiz" in pig Latin?

**8B** What is the plural of "ox"?

**10A** Which famous poet's name begins with "Words"?

**10B** In what kind of book can you look up the meanings of words?

**12A** To what does the word "lunar" refer?

**12B** What 6-letter word means "fit to eat"?

**14A** Marchpane is an old word for a kind of confectionery. What is it called nowadays?

**14B** What language is spoken in Jamaica?

**16A** Which word, meaning "a small stream", also means "to consume by fire"?

**16B** What does the French word *maison* mean?

# Buildings

**2A** *Prairie*.
**2B** He was an architect.

---

**4A** An estate agent.
**4B** Public House.

---

**6A** Norman.
**6B** A villa.

---

**8A** The roof. (It means an attic.)
**8B** A dormitory.

---

**10A** Brighton Pavilion.
**10B** Westminster Abbey.

---

**12A** Baker Street.
**12B** Sandringham.

---

**14A** The Vatican.
**14B** The Prime Minister's.

---

**16A** Cattle.
**16B** Dining room.

# Buildings

# Q

**2A** Laura Ingalls Wilder wrote about the *Little House on the*—what?

**2B** What was the occupation of Sir Christopher Wren?

**4A** Whose job is it to help you buy and sell your house?

**4B** What is the word "pub" short for?

**6A** Which of these architectural styles was the plainest—Baroque, Gothic, Norman or Perpendicular?

**6B** What is a house called in Spain?

**8A** In what part of a house might you find a garret?

**8B** What name is given to a room at boarding school in which many people sleep?

**10A** In 1782, the Prince Regent built an exotic edifice with several minarets and domes in a well-known sea-side town. What is it called?

**10B** Which London cathedral houses the Coronation Chair?

**12A** Sherlock Holmes's address was 221B, which street?

**12B** What is the name of the Queen's home in Norfolk?

**14A** In which famous palace would you find the Swiss Guard?

**14B** Whose official country home is called Chequers?

**16A** Who or what might live in a byre?

**16B** What does the French word *salle à manger* mean?

# I Say, I Say

2A  Karl Marx.

2B  Muhammad Ali (Cassius Clay).

---

4A  Pontius Pilate.

4B  Whiskas.

---

6A  Bugs Bunny's.

6B  Anne Boleyn.

---

8A  George Washington.

8B  "Come on down!"

---

10A  Michael Caine.

10B  Christmas (in Charles Dickens's *A Christmas Carol*).

---

12A  Africa.

12B  The Duke of Wellington (at the Battle of Waterloo).

---

14A  Coke. (Coca-Cola.)

14B  Ears.

---

16A  Peter Rabbit's mother.

16B  Paul Daniels'.

# I Say, I Say

**2A** Who said, "Workers of the world unite"—was it Karl Marx, Arthur Scargill or Wat Tyler?

**2B** Which boxer said, "I am the greatest"?

---

**4A** In the New Testament, who said, "I am innocent of the blood of this just person"?

**4B** Nine out of ten owners say their cats prefer it. What?

---

**6A** Whose catchphrase is "What's up, Doc"?

**6B** At the time of her execution, who said, "I have only a little neck"?

---

**8A** Who is supposed to have said, "I cannot tell a lie"?

**8B** What catchphrase is used in the TV show *The Price is Right*?

---

**10A** Which actor says, "Not a lot of people know that"?

**10B** On what occasion did Tiny Tim say, "God bless us every one!"?

---

**12A** In what continent did Sir Henry Morton Stanley say to Livingstone, "Dr Livingstone, I presume"?

**12B** Who is supposed to have said, "Up, Guards, and at 'em"?

---

**14A** It's the "real thing". What is it?

**14B** Mark Antony is supposed to have said, "Friends, Romans, countrymen, lend me your . . ."—what?

---

**16A** Who said, "Don't go into Mr McGregor's garden?"

**16B** Whose catchphrase is "Not a lot"?

# Pop Music

2A  The Shadows.

2B  The Rolling Stones.

---

4A  Sting.

4B  Stevie Wonder.

---

6A  David Essex.

6B  Electric Light Orchestra.

---

8A  Paul Gambaccini.

8B  Tina Turner.

---

10A  Ghostbusters.

10B  Bucks Fizz.

---

12A  Diana Ross.

12B  Wham.

---

14A  Alison Moyet.

14B  My blue suede shoes.

---

16A  George O'Dowd.

16B  They have all sung the title songs for James Bond films.

113

# Pop Music

**2A** What was Cliff Richard's backing group called?

**2B** Mick Jagger is the lead singer of which group?

---

**4A** Which pop star and actor got his nickname from the yellow and black sweater he used to wear?

**4B** Who joined Paul McCartney to sing "Ebony & Ivory"?

---

**6A** Which singer has the same name as an English county?

**6B** In the pop world, what do the initials E.L.O. stand for?

---

**8A** Which disc jockey has a name that means "little prawn"?

**8B** Who used to sing with her husband Ike?

---

**10A** According to the song, "Who you gonna call"?

**10B** Who won the Eurovision song contest with "Making Your Mind Up"?

---

**12A** Which famous singer started her career as lead singer with the Supremes?

**12B** George Michael and Andrew Ridgeley used to form a group called—what?

---

**14A** Which girl singer's name is an anagram of O NOISY METAL?

**14B** Elvis Presley sang "You can do what you like, but don't step on . . ."—what?

---

**16A** What is Boy George's real name?

**16B** Shirley Bassey, Sheena Easton, Tom Jones, Nancy Sinatra—what do these singers have in common?

2A  Pink.
2B  Skewbald.

---

4A  Green.
4B  White.

---

6A  Silver.
6B  Woad.

---

8A  Yellow.
8B  Red.

---

10A  Black.
10B  Orange.

---

12A  Yellow.
12B  A primary colour.

---

14A  Purple.
14B  Red.

---

16A  Yellow.
16B  Green.

# Colours

**2A** What colour was Princess Diana's going-away suit?

**2B** A brown and white horse is said to be—what?

---

**4A** What colour is associated with envy?

**4B** Jade can be green, pink or what?

---

**6A** What colour were Bobby Shaftoe's buckles?

**6B** Ancient Britons used to dye themselves blue. What was the dye called?

---

**8A** If you had jaundice, what colour would your skin be?

**8B** What colour is the rose of Lancaster?

---

**10A** In the Western world, what is the colour of mourning?

**10B** What colour is the ball at the top of a Belisha beacon?

---

**12A** Cowardice is associated with which colour?

**12B** What do you call a colour that cannot be produced by mixing other colours?

---

**14A** What colour is an aubergine?

**14B** The Swiss flag is a white cross on what colour ground?

---

**16A** In the song, what colour was the itsy bitsy, teeny weeny, polka dot bikini?

**16B** What colour uniforms do policemen in Northern Ireland wear?

# Myths & Legends

**2A** January (after Janus).
**2B** 100.

**4A** They melted.
**4B** A whirlpool (encountered by Odysseus).

**6A** Father Time.
**6B** The Golden Fleece.

**8A** Four.
**8B** Narcissus.

**10A** Mars.
**10B** The phoenix.

**12A** He had wings.
**12B** Because he was a god of wine.

**14A** Camelot.
**14B** Goat.

**16A** Snakes.
**16B** Twelve.

# Myths & Legends

**2A** What month is named after the Roman god of doorways and bridges?

**2B** How many eyes had Argus the watchman? Was it 1, 10, 100 or 1,000?

---

**4A** What happened to Icarus's wings when he flew too near the sun?

**4B** What was Charybdis—a whirlpool, a wind or a serpent?

---

**6A** Who is usually shown carrying a scythe and an hourglass?

**6B** What did Jason and the Argonauts set out to capture?

---

**8A** How many arms has the Hindu goddess Kali?

**8B** What spring flower is named after the Greek youth who fell in love with his own reflection?

---

**10A** What was the name of the Roman god of war?

**10B** Which Arabian bird set fire to itself and rose anew from the ashes every five hundred years?

---

**12A** What was unusual about the mythical horse Pegasus?

**12B** Why is the god Bacchus often shown with grapes?

---

**14A** According to legend, what was the name of King Arthur's castle?

**14B** Pan was part man and part—which animal?

---

**16A** What did Medusa have on her head instead of hair?

**16B** How many labours did Hercules have to carry out?

# Food & Drink

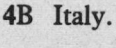 **A**

**2A** Edam.

**2B** The seeds of a tree.

**4A** It has three or more slices of toast or bread.

**4B** Italy.

**6A** Curry.

**6B** Steak.

**8A** The stomach lining.

**8B** Melon.

**10A** Sugar cane.

**10B** Sukiyaki.

**12A** Jello.

**12B** Sausages.

**14A** A teacake.

**14B** The potato.

**16A** A water ice.

**16B** On a menu.

2A What is the name of the Dutch cheese that has a bright red rind?

2B Does cocoa come from the seeds of a tree, a root, or from nuts?

4A What is special about a club sandwich?

4B With which country is spaghetti chiefly associated?

6A What gives mulligatawny soup its hot flavour?

6B Tournedos, entrecôte and T-bone are all types of —what?

8A What part of the cow is tripe?

8B Ogen, honeydew and cantaloupe are all types of —what?

0A Is rum made from sugar cane, banana, cocoa beans or pimentos?

0B A famous Japanese dish—is it sukiyaki, harakiri or origami?

2A What do Americans call jelly?

2B Toad in the hole consists of what, cooked in batter?

4A What is a Sally Lunn—a variety of potato, a teacake, or a type of pie?

4B Which very common vegetable was first introduced to this country by Sir Walter Raleigh?

6A What is another name for a sorbet?

6B Where might you find the expressions *à la carte* and *table d'hôte*?

# Animals

**2A** Guinea pig.
**2B** Three.

---

**4A** Duck.
**4B** China.

---

**6A** A chicken.
**6B** Because they kill snakes.

---

**8A** A nanny goat.
**8B** Dog.

---

**10A** The common frog.
**10B** A tiger.

---

**12A** A golden retriever.
**12B** A stoat.

---

**14A** It has no tail.
**14B** A horse.

---

**16A** Whale.
**16B** The hippopotamus.

# Animals

2A  What is another name for a cavy?

2B  How many hearts has an octopus?

---

4A  Mallard, Aylesbury and Muscovy are all types of —what?

4B  Pekinese dogs came originally from which country?

---

6A  What type of creature is a Buff Orpington?

6B  Many years ago, in India, it was common for households to keep a pet mongoose. Why?

---

8A  What is a female goat called?

8B  Is a Rhodesian ridgeback a breed of horse, a pig or a dog?

---

10A  It's 7 cm long, olive-green, has long legs, hibernates, is amphibious, and eats insects. What is it?

10B  What type of animal is Shere Khan in *The Jungle Book*?

---

12A  What breed is Goldie, the dog who belongs to *Blue Peter* presenter Simon Groom?

12B  In the winter it grows a white fur coat known as ermine. What is it?

---

14A  What is unusual about a Manx cat?

14B  A Percheron is a breed of what animal?

---

16A  Humpback, cachalot, right and killer are all types of—what?

16B  What animal is known as the river horse?

# Television

**2A** Wrestling.
**2B** Pointed ears.

---

**4A** Denver, Colorado.
**4B** Mrs McCluskey.

---

**6A** Ken Barlow.
**6B** Bad attitude. (He was described like this in the army.)

---

**8A** Wilma.
**8B** Kenny Everett's.

---

**10A** *The Colbys*.
**10B** Thomas.

---

**12A** Jersey.
**12B** Darts.

---

**14A** A witch (in *The Pink Windmill Show*).
**14B** K.I.T.T.

---

**16A** Jellystone.
**16B** They're all
weather forecasters.

# Television

**2A** On which sport does Kent Walton commentate?

**2B** Mr Spock in *Star Trek* has a distinctive physical feature. What is it?

---

**4A** In which American city is the soap opera *Dynasty* set?

**4B** What is the name of the headmistress of Grange Hill?

---

**6A** Which character has been in *Coronation Street* right from the beginning?

**6B** One of the A-team is called B.A. What do these initials stand for?

---

**8A** In *The Flintstones*, what is Fred's wife's name?

**8B** Whose show is always in "the best possible taste"?

---

**10A** In which TV series does Sable appear?

**10B** What is Magnum's Christian name?

---

**12A** On what island is the *Bergerac* series set?

**12B** Which sport is featured in *Bullseye*?

---

**14A** Who or what is Grotbags?

**14B** In *Knight Rider*, what is the name of Michael Knight's car?

---

**16A** In which National Park does Yogi Bear live?

**16B** Willis, McCaskill, Kettley and Fish—what do they have in common?

# Mixed Bag

**2A** Dick Francis.
**2B** The speed of a ship.

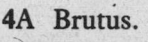

**4A** Brutus.
**4B** Oxfam.

**6A** *Jaws*.
**6B** Save Our Souls.

**8A** Dancer.
**8B** Russian (Valentina Tereshkova).

**10A** None.
**10B** C.

**12A** Quasimodo.
**12B** The ballpoint pen.

**14A** Birmingham.
**14B** Cock Robin.

**16A** A printing press.
**16B** Apples.

# Mixed Bag

**2A** Which ex-jockey became a famous writer of detective stories?

**2B** What is measured in knots?

---

**4A** Who killed Julius Caesar? Was it Nero, Brutus, Mark Antony or Claudius?

**4B** What name is normally used for the Oxford Committee for Famine Relief?

---

**6A** In which film is Robert Shaw eaten by a "great white"?

**6B** What does the distress signal "S.O.S." stand for?

---

**8A** Actor, singer, composer, writer, dancer, pianist—which of these words does not apply to Noel Coward?

**8B** What nationality was the first woman space traveller?

---

**10A** How many strings has a jew's harp?

**10B** What is the roman symbol for one hundred?

---

**12A** Who was the Hunchback of Notre Dame?

**12B** What did Ladislao and Georg Biro invent?

---

**14A** Where do Brummies come from?

**14B** In the nursery rhyme, who was killed by a sparrow?

---

**16A** Did William Caxton invent a printing press, a cure for smallpox, a weaving loom or an early lawnmower?

**16B** What is cider made from?

Use bookmarks to help you remember which quiz you have reached.

**The first player to reach the centre is the winner.**

## For more than 2 players

Each player chooses a number, as before, but there should be as many odd numbers as even. This way, the players with odd numbers ask questions of those with even numbers, and vice versa. They thus don't get to see their own answers.

# How to play an exciting quiz game with this book

The object of the game is to be the first to reach the middle of the book. Players ask each other questions from both the back and front of the book. The answers can be found on the back of each question page.

Each player should have a bookmark.

## For two players
One player chooses an **odd** number between 1 and 15, and answers questions from the **front** of the book.

The other player chooses an **even** number between 2 and 16, and answers questions from the **back** of the book.

Toss a coin to see who should begin.

- Players answer **only** the questions that bear the number they have chosen.
- Work from the outside of the book towards the centre.
- When a player answers a question correctly, he has another turn.
- When a player answers a question incorrectly, his turn is over.

* If a player answers an "A" question correctly, he goes straight on to the next quiz.
* If a player answers an "A" question incorrectly, he stays on the same quiz and tries to answer the "B" question on his next turn.
* If a player answers a "B" question correctly, he goes straight on to the next quiz.
* If a player answers a "B" question incorrectly, he goes on to the next quiz on his next turn.